LIGHT SAUCES

LIGHT SAUCES

Delicious Low-Calorie, Low-Fat, Low-Cholesterol Recipes For Meats and Fish, Pasta, Salads, Vegetables, and Desserts

BARRY BLUESTEIN and KEVIN MORRISSEY

CONTEMPORARY
BOOKS

CHICAGO

Library of Congress Cataloging-in-Publication Data

Bluestein, Barry.
    Light sauces : delicious low-calorie, low-fat, low cholesterol
recipes / Barry Bluestein and Kevin Morrissey.
       p.   cm.
    Includes index.
    ISBN 0-8092-4063-7 (pbk.)
    1. Low-calorie diet—Recipes.   2. Low-fat diet—Recipes.   3.Low-
cholesterol diet—Recipes.   4. Sauces.   I. Morrissey, Kevin.
II. Title.
RM222.2.B5867   1991
641.5′635—dc20   90-27622
                                                      CIP

Published by Contemporary Books, Inc.
180 North Michigan Avenue, Chicago, Illinois 60601
Manufactured in the United States of America
International Standard Book Number: 0-8092-4063-7

Dedicated to the memory of Mitchell R. Cutler, who always had faith in books and in us.

CONTENTS

ACKNOWLEDGMENTS

We wish to gratefully acknowledge the ongoing assistance of Elaine Barlas, whose support, insight, and advice have been offered generously since our paths first crossed.

Special thanks are due Rob Humrickhouse, with whom we spent many a late night "birthing the baby" that was to become Season To Taste Books. Rob was always there with an encouraging word or an extra paintbrush when we really needed him. Thanks to Kathleen Rybak, Patty Oria, and Claudia Clark Potter for their support of our business and of our writing; and to our editor, Linda Gray.

And last but never least, we raise our whisks in a salute to Cecelia "Cis" Hartman, without whose gracious help and boundless knowledge this book, like so many of our projects, could not have been accomplished.

FOREWORD

What's sauce for the goose is sauce for the gander, as our grandmothers used to say. That is, unless either is counting calories, on a restricted diet, or simply attempting to prepare light, healthful meals—in which case there is often no sauce anywhere in sight.

Dieters have long been told to simply do without sauces, since most are typically so high in calories. And anyone on a heart-healthy or low-cholesterol diet was likewise conditioned to view sauces, usually laden with fat and cholesterol, as the forbidden fruit of the dining table. The few sauces that do grace the pages of health-conscious cookbooks are, more often than not, unappealing, uninspired, and limited in use.

Indeed, sauces represent something of a quandary in an era of informed, health-conscious cooking. For centuries, cooks have used sauces to enhance the flavor, texture, and appearance of the foods we eat. Yet today's cook has come to associate sauces solely with the intricate and rich accompaniments of traditional French cuisine, or with the equally fattening and artery-hardening gravies that were a staple of American home cooking in the not-too-distant past.

Our goal is to restore sauces to their rightful place in the culinary repertoire of the times and to demonstrate how easily sauces can be a part of healthy eating. No longer need dinnertime be a barren and joyless confrontation with dry, tasteless morsels of food staring up from spartan plates. With *Light Sauces*, you can control your calorie, fat, and cholesterol consumption without sacrificing the flavor enhancement and finishing touch that only a sauce can lend.

The key to "svelte saucing" is quite simply an emphasis on lighter ingredients, such as colorful fruit and vegetable purees, savory herbs and spices, and low-fat or nonfat dairy products, along with avoidance (wherever possible) of the starches and animal fats that have, unfortunately, been the mainstay of old-fashioned sauces.

In *Light Sauces*, you will find sauces for poultry, seafood, meats, pasta, vegetables, and fruit; sauces for appetizers, entrees, side dishes, and desserts; and salad dressings, marinades, salsas, and chutneys. Each recipe includes calorie, fat, and cholesterol counts, along with recommendations for dishes that the sauce will accompany best, serving suggestions, and tips on refrigerator or freezer shelf life.

We've also included an introductory chapter on ingredients, equipment, and techniques for preparing sauces, with tips on shopping, informed label reading, timesaving use of appliances, and basic cooking methods. As many sauces call for the inclusion of a stock, we provide recipes for tasty, low-fat homemade chicken and beef stocks as well.

All of the delicious sauces, dressings, and toppings in this book are versatile and easy to make. They complete any dish, enhancing its appearance, texture, and, most important, taste, and can turn the humblest of meals into a special occasion. Our sauces provide a refreshing change from the starchy, heavy concoctions of yesterday and a healthier and far superior alternative to any prepackaged product available.

We offer this book in retaliation for every dry, bland, and flavorless scrap of food that has ever reared its sorry shadow over the pursuit of a healthful diet—and in celebration of the true gastronomical delight of saucing!

1
INTRODUCTION

With *Light Sauces* we hope to make light, healthy saucing an integral part of everyday meal preparation for the health-conscious cook. This is not intended as a diet book, although it can be used successfully by dieters. Our primary goal is to present an appealing array of sauces, all low in calories and fat content, that are made with healthful and readily available ingredients and that can be prepared as easily and quickly as possible.

We provide recipes for sauces to accompany a wide range of foods, including but by no means limited to the broiled chicken, fish, or lean meat that form the cornerstone of most diet regimens. We also include sauces that will enhance shrimp, pasta, red meat, and desserts. Our aim is versatility, and we leave to you the determination of what foods our sauces will grace.

Calorie counts for each recipe are presented per tablespoon, allowing you to determine desired serving size and readily calculate calories per serving. The strict dieter may wish to limit serving size to a single tablespoon, while others can adjust portions knowledgeably according to their own desired calorie intake.

To further help sound dietary planning, grams of fat are also presented per tablespoon, as are milligrams of cholesterol. While we did not set out to write a low-cholesterol cookbook, we found that most of our recipes *are* low in cholesterol (many are cholesterol-free) and so have included this count to assist individuals on a cholesterol-restricted diet.

Calorie, fat, and cholesterol counts are rounded off to the nearest tenth of a percent. In calculating all counts, we considered trace quantities (those less than one-tenth of 1 percent) of calories, fat, or cholesterol present in any ingredient as zero. Counts do not account for any additional garnishes that may be suggested in recipe introductions or any food with which you may pair the sauce.

Recipes call for measured quantities of

minced, chopped, or diced ingredients, which allows for more accurate counts, but include equivalents to help you shop (e.g., we will call for 1 cup chopped white onion, which is the approximate end result of chopping one medium-sized white onion). When recipes call for inclusion of ingredients in some form that is not readily measured (such as a pepper that is to be pureed or a tomato cut in quarters), counts are based on a whole ingredient of average size.

HOW THIS BOOK IS ORGANIZED

Chapters 2 through 5 are organized around the ingredient that provides the principal flavor to each sauce. These sauces are intended to accompany poultry, fish and shellfish, meats, pasta, and vegetables, as suggested in each recipe. They can be used with full portions served as entrees or, in many cases, with smaller portions served as first courses or as part of a buffet or grazing table. We note where any sauce will work especially well with an appetizer.

Chapter 2 includes recipes for variations on the theme of the venerable tomato-based sauce, including svelte renditions of pizza and barbecue sauce—but without the excessive quantities of oil and butter that add unwanted fat and calories.

The sauces in chapter 3 derive their character from herbs and spices, ranging from subtle tarragon, dill, and basil to pungent curries and dried chili peppers. The bases for some of these sauces are our own versions of the traditional white sauce, made with skim milk instead of whole milk or cream and thickened with very small amounts of potato starch or cornstarch mixed with dry nonfat milk powder instead of flour. Others are based on svelte adaptations of the classic roux, with just enough butter to impart flavor and flour to thicken.

Chapter 4 consists of recipes for savory fruit-flavored sauces that make wonderful accompaniments to meats and poultry, as distinguished from their sweeter relatives, which are used to top desserts. Many of the sauces in this chapter are thickened with fruit purees. We also make use of the natural and convenient spreadable fruit products that have come onto the market in recent years.

The sauces in chapter 5 are flavored by members of the vegetable kingdom, some solely, some in consort with other vegetables when the flavors meld to produce a distinctive taste. Many of these recipes call for preparation of simple purees, augmented with a hint of seasoning for highlight.

Chapters 6 through 8 are of a somewhat more specialized nature. Chapter 6 offers recipes for dressings for green salads, cold veggies, fruit, and cold poultry and fish. Chapter 7 consists of what we call "sidelines and building blocks." Here we include recipes for favored accompaniments such as salsas and chutneys, which can't be labeled sauces in the strictest definition of the term, and for homemade versions of the stocks called for in many of our recipes. Chapter 8 is a tempting medley of sumptuous yet light dessert sauces, the only fitting note on which to end the book.

INGREDIENTS

Sauces should be pleasing both to the eye and to the palate, an objective best achieved by using the freshest of ingredients. In some cases, there is simply no substitution that will work—where a fresh herb or spice supplies the primary flavor of a sauce, for example, or imbues it with a distinctive color. This holds true where only the crunchiness of fresh ingredients will lend texture to a salsa, where only the taste of a fresh tomato will do in an uncooked tomato sauce, where only a fresh vegetable or fruit will result in a truly outstanding puree.

We recognize, however, that it isn't necessary to start completely from scratch in all cases. Therefore, we use canned or frozen products when their use will simplify preparation considerably without compromising the taste, texture, or appearance of the sauce—or when the fresh variety may not be available year-round. The option to use dried herbs is given whenever the sauce won't be compromised, and dried herbs are specifically called for when quantities are very small.

Carefully reading product labels is crucial when the motivations of health and convenience intersect. Most, but not all, manufacturers voluntarily list nutritional information on those products that are low in calories, fat, and cholesterol. Products packed in water or in natural, unsweetened juices are readily labeled as such.

Be aware that vast differences exist even among the products so labeled. For example, canned fruits packed in water contain substantially fewer calories than the same fruits packed in natural juice (which are, needless to say, much lower in calories than fruits packed in syrup).

We call for use of only those products that are available in most large supermarkets; you shouldn't have to search out esoteric brands in health-food stores to stay within our guidelines. Our calorie counts are based upon the lowest-calorie products readily available. Read labels carefully (including the fine print) and compare calorie counts among brands.

As we give the option for using canned or

homemade when recipes call for inclusion of stock, counts are based on the lowest-calorie commercial products readily available.

Here are some tips on what to look for when obtaining and prepping specific ingredients:

We use small amounts of natural, flavorful *butter*, which is no higher in calories than most substitutes and which we think tastes better. If you want to further reduce your cholesterol intake, however, substitute margarine or one of the butter/margarine blends.

Canned fruit generally should be purchased packed in water. Fruit not readily available packed in water should be purchased packed in natural, unsweetened juice. If you use fruit packed in syrup, rinse it thoroughly under cold running water before using.

Canned vegetables should also be purchased packed in water. Any other variety you may use should be thoroughly rinsed under cold running water.

When using *fresh milk* (some of our recipes call for skim milk or buttermilk), be sure to check the freshness expiration date on the carton. Do not store sauces that contain milk beyond this date.

In many recipes, we give the option of using *frozen fruit* instead of fresh, for convenience and to make sure that you can enjoy these recipes year-round. Always use the unsweetened varieties.

We specify the use of fresh or dried *herbs* in each recipe—fresh when it is important to the integrity of the sauce, either/or when interchangeable, and dried when the herbs are used in very small quantities. Know that you can always substitute fresh for dried (one tablespoon of fresh herbs is the equivalent of one teaspoon of dried herbs), but that using dried when fresh herbs are called for could impair the flavor and color of the sauce.

When using prepared *horseradish*, always squeeze out excess water before adding to the recipe.

Remember the pungency of *hot peppers*. Carefully follow precautionary notes for prepping, as contact with pepper seeds, veins, or juice can cause serious eye and skin irritation. Also beware that, in terms of taste, they pack quite a kick.

Many of our recipes call for *lemon juice*, which we suggest always be freshly squeezed. The added zest is well worth the little bit of extra effort. *Orange juice* may be freshly squeezed, from a carton, or from a concentrate as you wish, but should always be unsweetened.

We do use small quantities of *oil*, particularly for sautéing. A few recipes call for the unique flavor of olive oil, in which case at least virgin quality should be used. All other recipes using oil call for canola oil, a vegetable oil derived from the rapeseed plant that is readily available in supermarkets. Although there is little difference in calories among most oils, canola oil is as low in saturated fats as olive oil and imparts almost no flavor of its own.

When a recipe calls for *soy sauce*, be sure to use a variety that contains wheat as well as soybeans, as these are the lowest in calories and fat.

When recipes call for *stock*, you may use either canned or homemade. We prefer the taste and freshness of homemade, as well as the ability to control fat content during preparation, so we include our own recipes for homemade beef and chicken stocks. If using canned, spoon the coagulated fat off the top of the stock after opening.

Other than when fresh *tomatoes* are specifically called for, we recommend using canned tomatoes, unless you grow your own or are lucky enough to have a source for buying fresh off the vine. The canned variety has been allowed to ripen longer on the vine and has a higher nutritional content than supermarket-variety hothouse tomatoes, which are picked before they've fully ripened.

Always use plain nonfat *yogurt* in our recipes (not low-fat, and *certainly* not vanilla). Check the freshness expiration date on the carton, and do not store sauces containing yogurt beyond this date. We do not recommend freezing any sauces that contain yogurt.

EQUIPMENT

Saucing requires a minimum of kitchen equipment:

A *grater* that allows for fine or coarse grating of peel.

Good-quality chopping and paring *knives* for prepping of fruits and vegetables. (Trust us, avoiding wasted time and frustration is well worth the initial investment in quality knives).

Nonreactive *mixing bowls* in a variety of sizes. Glass, enamel, or china bowls will do nicely. Avoid metal bowls, as the interaction of metal with acidic ingredients can affect the taste and color of the sauce.

A supply of sandwich-sized *plastic bags* that can be tightly sealed, in which to freeze portions of sauce and stocks for use long into the future. (We suggest freezing in ¼-cup, ½-cup, or cup quantities, from which servings and calorie counts are easily calculated.)

Airtight *plastic storage containers* in which to keep sauces fresh and free of neighboring odors in the refrigerator, and to ensure safe refrigeration of stocks and stock-based sauces.

A *potato masher* for pureeing various ingredients by hand.

A *rubber scraper* or *spatula* for transferring mixtures from bowl to pan to food processor, etc. (More than one comes in very handy, unless you're particularly adept at washing utensils between steps of a recipe.)

Nonreactive *saucepans* (such as enamel, stainless steel, or glass) in a variety of sizes. While a medium-sized saucepan will do for most recipes, we call for a small saucepan when a very small amount of liquid, which should not be spread over too large a surface, is called for, and for a large saucepan for higher-yield recipes. Heavy-bottomed (copper- or enamel-clad) saucepans are recommended when care must be taken not to burn the mixture being heated.

A heavy-bottomed *skillet* for recipes where the mixture being heated is best distributed over a larger cooking surface so that more liquid is exposed and thickening is thus hastened.

A *stockpot* for the preparation of stocks, preferably a large heavy-bottomed one that will allow for even distribution of heat and will enable you to make large quantities of stock that can be frozen in portions for future use. It's a bonus if your stockpot is nonstick coated, as this aids in the browning of bones.

Strainers, including a colander for draining and rinsing and a fine-mesh sieve for straining finer particles.

Finally, a *whisk* and a *wooden spoon*, preferably more than one of each, as you'll use both constantly in preparing sauces.

Electronic kitchen gadgets are in a class by themselves; in saucing, as in most culinary endeavors, many are well worth their proverbial weight in gold.

The *food processor*, which allows for considerable control in achieving desired size in procedures such as chunking or dicing, is truly a cook's best friend when it comes to pureeing. (Using a food processor or blender is the only way to puree many fruits.) In fact, we recommend having two food processors; a standard size for big jobs and a mini for such functions as mincing garlic or chopping small quantities of onion.

For all of our recipes, fit your food processor with the standard steel blade; special cutting and slicing disks are not needed.

The trusty old *blender* can also help with many functions, but it really works best with liquid rather than solid ingredients. If you're pureeing in the blender, be careful not to make a paste. Because the blender is taller than it is wide, the food at the top won't be pureed unless it is pushed down (with a wooden spoon, every few seconds while the machine is turned off), and the food at the bottom will quickly turn to paste.

TECHNIQUE

Timing is critical in making sauces. Whenever we call for a specific result (sauté to a certain consistency, thicken, etc.) that will be achieved within a few minutes or less, we purposefully list the desired result first and the approximate cooking time second. You will need to watch the sauce carefully. No two stoves are alike, and what takes 2 minutes on our stove could take 1½ or 2½ on yours.

With electric stoves, it takes time for changes in burner temperature. You may need to allow a little extra cooking time when the recipe calls for raising the heat, or remove the pan from the burner for a few seconds while it cools down when the recipe calls for reducing the heat.

When *sautéing* (usually done over medium heat in a liquid that has been preheated), always stir the ingredients constantly.

Unless otherwise specified, *simmering* should be done uncovered, which allows excess liquid to vaporize, thus thickening the mixture. Covering traps the vapor, which turns back into liquid.

Approximate cooking times are more crucial to thickening, which is a somewhat subjective term depending upon the individual sauce. In general, "thick" means a consistency that will coat a wooden spoon or that will form a track on the surface when stirred.

2
TOMATO SAUCES

BASIC TOMATO SAUCE
TOMATO FRESCA SAUCE
HOMEMADE MARINARA SAUCE
SAUCE CREOLE
SAUCE DIABLO
SASSY COCKTAIL SAUCE
QUICK BARBECUE SAUCE
CHILI BARBECUE SAUCE
PIZZA SAUCE

BASIC TOMATO SAUCE

1 tablespoon virgin olive oil
1 16-ounce can peeled tomatoes, drained
⅛ teaspoon black pepper
1 bay leaf
½ tablespoon chopped fresh basil or ½ teaspoon dried basil

Makes about 2 cups

Calories per tablespoon: 6.7
Fat per tablespoon: 0.5 g.
Cholesterol per tablespoon: 0

If you're lucky enough to have a source for homegrown tomatoes, they may by all means be substituted for canned. To peel and seed fresh tomatoes: Make an X at the blossom on the bottom of the tomato with a sharp knife. Put into boiling water (tomatoes will sink at first) and cook 2–3 minutes until tomatoes rise to the top. Remove, taking care not to burn yourself, and run under cold water. The X will have opened so that you can peel back each quarter of skin with a knife, as you would an orange. Cut tomatoes into quarters and squeeze out seeds.

Heat oil for about 30 seconds in a heavy-bottomed saucepan over medium heat. Add tomatoes, black pepper, bay leaf, and basil. Turn heat down to low. Simmer uncovered, periodically stirring and breaking up tomatoes with the side of a wooden spoon, for 15 to 20 minutes, until thickened. Make sure to remove bay leaf before serving. Serve immediately.

Suggested pairings: fish and shellfish, chicken and other poultry, pasta

This sauce may be stored in the refrigerator for up to five days, or in the freezer for up to six months.

Note: As with any cooked tomato sauce, be sure to let this cool before refrigerating or freezing, or the tomatoes will give off water, causing the sauce to separate.

TOMATO FRESCA SAUCE

2 cups diced fresh tomato (about 2
    tomatoes)
1½ teaspoons minced garlic (about
    2 cloves)
⅛ teaspoon salt
¼ teaspoon dried oregano
1 tablespoon finely chopped fresh
    basil or 1 teaspoon dried basil
¾ teaspoon canola oil

Makes about 2 cups

Calories per tablespoon: 2.9
Fat per tablespoon: 0.1 g.
Cholesterol per tablespoon: 0

A light, refreshing sauce that graces vegetables or pasta equally well. This recipe can easily be cut in half.

Thoroughly mix together tomatoes, garlic, salt, oregano, and basil. Add oil and mix in thoroughly. Serve at room temperature.

Suggested pairings: pasta, spaghetti squash, bean sprouts

This sauce may be stored in the refrigerator for one day.

HOMEMADE MARINARA SAUCE

1 tablespoon virgin olive oil
¾ cup coarsely chopped white
   onion (about 1 small onion)
2 teaspoons finely minced garlic
   (2–3 cloves)
1 16-ounce can peeled tomatoes,
   drained (liquid reserved)
1 tablespoon tomato paste
½ teaspoon red wine vinegar
1 tablespoon chopped fresh basil
   or 1 teaspoon dried basil
1 teaspoon dried oregano
⅛ teaspoon black pepper

Makes about 2 cups

Calories per tablespoon: 9.0
Fat per tablespoon: 0.5 g.
Cholesterol per tablespoon: 0

As its name connotes, marinara sauce was created to feed passengers on sea voyages. It's a hearty and substantial alternative to meat sauces. We think you'll find that this slightly chunky version works as well on land as at sea, and that it is equally at home atop an entree or a side dish of pasta.

Heat oil for about 30 seconds in a heavy-bottomed saucepan over medium-low heat. Add onion and garlic. Lightly sauté until onion is soft and slightly translucent, taking care not to burn (about 2 minutes). Add tomatoes. Sauté another 1 to 2 minutes over medium heat, breaking up the tomatoes with the side of a wooden spoon. Add reserved liquid. Mix in tomato paste, then add red wine vinegar, basil, oregano, and black pepper. Bring to a boil over medium heat. Turn heat down to low and simmer uncovered for about 20 minutes, until thickened, stirring occasionally. Serve immediately.

Suggested pairings: chicken, pork, pasta

This sauce may be stored in the refrigerator for up to five days, or in the freezer for up to six months.

Note: Be sure to let sauce cool before refrigerating or freezing, or the tomatoes will give off water and cause the sauce to separate.

SAUCE CREOLE

1 tablespoon canola oil

1 cup chopped white onion (about 1 medium onion)

2 teaspoons chopped garlic (2–3 cloves)

½ cup minced green bell pepper (about ½ pepper)

½ cup minced red bell pepper (about ½ pepper)

1 16-ounce can Italian plum tomatoes, drained

15 large pitted unstuffed green olives, chopped

¼ teaspoon cayenne pepper

1½ tablespoons chopped fresh thyme or 1½ teaspoons dried thyme

1 tablespoon tomato paste

Makes about 3 cups

Calories per tablespoon: 8.3
Fat per tablespoon: 0.5 g.
Cholesterol per tablespoon: 0

This zesty sauce brings a little bit of old New Orleans to a range of main courses and side dishes.

Heat oil in a large heavy-bottomed saucepan for about 30 seconds over medium heat. Add onion, garlic, green pepper, and red pepper. Sauté until onion turns translucent (about 2 to 3 minutes). Add tomatoes, breaking them up with the side of a wooden spoon, and olives. Add cayenne pepper and thyme. Stir in tomato paste. Simmer uncovered over medium-low heat for 10 minutes. Serve immediately.

Suggested pairings: chicken, fish, ground meat, spaghetti squash, rice, warmed peppers

This sauce may be stored in the refrigerator for up to five days, or in the freezer for up to six months.

Note: Be sure to let sauce cool before refrigerating or freezing, or the tomatoes will give off water and cause the sauce to separate.

SAUCE DIABLO

1 tablespoon canola oil
¼ cup chopped white onion (about
⅓ small onion)
¼ cup chopped celery (about 1
medium stalk)
1 teaspoon minced garlic (1–1½
cloves)
⅛ teaspoon ground cloves
1 cup peeled, seeded, and chopped
fresh tomato (about 1 tomato)
2 tablespoons tomato paste
½ tablespoon hot sauce

Makes about 1½ cups

Calories per tablespoon: 7.0
Fat per tablespoon: 0.5 g.
Cholesterol per tablespoon: 0

We prefer fresh tomatoes in this versatile sauce, but canned may be substituted. Remember that fresh tomatoes can be peeled, seeded, chopped, and frozen in 1-cup packages for easy use out of season.

Heat oil in a heavy-bottomed frying pan for about 30 seconds over medium heat. Add onion, celery, garlic, and cloves. Sauté until celery softens (3 to 5 minutes), taking care not to burn garlic. Stir in tomato, tomato paste, and hot sauce. Simmer 10 minutes uncovered over medium-low heat. Serve immediately.

Suggested pairings: meats, chicken, fish, shrimp, steamed lobster, other shellfish, steamed vegetables

This sauce may be stored in the refrigerator for up to five days, or in the freezer for up to six months.

Note: Be sure to let sauce cool before refrigerating or freezing, or the tomatoes will give off water and cause the sauce to separate.

SASSY COCKTAIL SAUCE

¾ cup reduced-calorie catsup
2 tablespoons prepared
   horseradish
⅛ teaspoon hot sauce
⅛ teaspoon freshly squeezed lemon
   juice

Makes about 1 cup

Calories per tablespoon: 6.8
Fat per tablespoon: 0
Cholesterol per tablespoon: 0

This smooth but perky rendition of the classic red sauce for fish and shellfish will enliven many an appetizer as well. Try it with radishes or with trimmed scallions.

Combine all ingredients in a bowl and mix thoroughly. Serve at room temperature or chilled (cover if chilling).

Suggested pairings: shrimp, crab, clams, oysters

This sauce may be stored in the refrigerator for up to one week.

QUICK BARBECUE SAUCE

¼ cup reduced-calorie catsup
¼ cup chili sauce
2 teaspoons stone-ground mustard
2 tablespoons Worcestershire
   sauce
1 tablespoon red wine vinegar
⅛ teaspoon cayenne pepper
⅛ teaspoon dark brown sugar
2 cloves garlic

Makes about ¾ cup

Calories per tablespoon: 12.1
Fat per tablespoon: 0
Cholesterol per tablespoon: 0

This lively sauce can be made in minutes since it doesn't require any cooking at all. Just spread it over poultry or meat before baking, broiling, or grilling. For a novel appetizer, pour over cream cheese and serve with crackers as a spread.

Stir catsup, chili sauce, mustard, Worcestershire sauce, vinegar, cayenne pepper, and brown sugar together in a bowl. Crush in garlic, using a garlic press, and stir. Use at room temperature.

Suggested pairings: chicken, pork, beef ribs

This sauce may be stored in the refrigerator for up to five days, or in the freezer for up to six months.

CHILI BARBECUE SAUCE

2 tablespoons chopped white onion
 (less than ¼ small onion)
1½ teaspoons minced garlic (about
 2 cloves)
¼ cup white vinegar
¼ cup tomato paste
¼ cup water
1 teaspoon Dijon-style mustard
1 teaspoon Worcestershire sauce
¼ teaspoon ground cumin
1½ teaspoons chili powder

_____

Makes about ⅔ cup

Calories per tablespoon: 7.2
Fat per tablespoon: 0.1 g.
Cholesterol per tablespoon: 0

The chili taste is pervasive in this cooked barbecue sauce. For a snack, try serving with baked taco chips.

Place onion, garlic, and vinegar in saucepan and bring to a low boil over medium heat. Continue to cook until the quantity of liquid in the pan is reduced by half (about 5 minutes). Whisk in tomato paste, then water. Whisk in remaining ingredients. Serve immediately.

Suggested pairings: beef patty, turkey patty, wieners, Polish sausage

This sauce may be stored in the refrigerator for up to five days, or in the freezer for up to six months.

PIZZA SAUCE

1 tablespoon canola oil
⅓ cup finely chopped white onion
   (about ⅓ medium onion)
1 large clove garlic
1 16-ounce can crushed tomatoes,
   not drained
2 tablespoons tomato paste
½ teaspoon dried basil
½ teaspoon dried oregano
¼ teaspoon sugar

Makes about 1⅓ cups

Calories per tablespoon: 14.9
Fat per tablespoon: 0.9 g.
Cholesterol per tablespoon: 0

This sauce can be frozen in small quantities to have on hand for quick, individual low-calorie pizzas.

Heat oil in heavy-bottomed saucepan over medium-low heat for about 30 seconds. Add onion. Crush in garlic, using a garlic press. Sauté until onion is translucent (3 to 5 minutes). Add remaining ingredients and stir well. Bring to a boil. Turn heat down to low and simmer uncovered for 50 to 60 minutes, stirring periodically to prevent scorching, until mixture is a thick but spreadable consistency. Let cool. Use at room temperature.

Suggested pairings: To make individual pizzas, take a 6-inch round of pita bread, split horizontally to form two rounds, and toast. Spread 2–3 tablespoons pizza sauce on each. Top with steamed vegetables and sprinkle lightly with grated mozzarella cheese. Bake at 350 degrees for 8 to 10 minutes, until cheese melts and vegetables are warm.

This sauce may be stored in the refrigerator for up to three days, or in the freezer for up to six months.

3
HERBED AND SPICED SAUCES

RED CHILI SAUCE
ROSEMARY LIME SAUCE
DILL SAUCE
HORSERADISH SAUCE
TARRAGON MUSTARD SAUCE
TARRAGON BUTTER SAUCE
BASIL BUTTER SAUCE
GARLIC MUSTARD SAUCE
CURRY SAUCE
CREAMY CURRY SAUCE
SPICY DIPPING SAUCE
WASABI SAUCE

RED CHILI SAUCE

6 large dried ancho chili peppers
Boiling water to cover peppers
 (about 6 cups)
2 large cloves garlic, cut into
 quarters
½ teaspoon ground cumin
1 teaspoon dried oregano
½ cup warm water

Makes about 2 cups

Calories per tablespoon: 4.0
Fat per tablespoon: 0
Cholesterol per tablespoon: 0

A little reminiscent of the Mexican mole sauce (but without the chocolate), this sauce works well baked on an entree, ladled over a fully cooked dish, or as a base to be topped by a crab cake or fish cake. Be sure to follow the precautions noted in the directions for handling hot peppers.

Place chili peppers in a large bowl and cover with boiling water. Cover bowl tightly with a plate or pot lid and let stand about 1 hour, until peppers are soft and plump. Wearing rubber gloves, remove the stem from each chili and break open the pod over the bowl. Remove all seeds and veins from inside. Swish pods in the soaking water or hold under cold running water to be sure they are free of seeds. Cut each pod into four to six slices. Place slices in the bowl of a food processor or blender. Add garlic, cumin, oregano, and warm water. Puree to a smooth consistency. Warm thoroughly in an uncovered saucepan over low heat 2 to 3 minutes, stirring occasionally. Serve immediately.

Suggested pairings: chicken, pork, monkfish, baked potato

This sauce may be stored in the refrigerator for up to five days.

ROSEMARY LIME SAUCE

¾ cup chicken stock
2 tablespoons chopped scallion
(about 1–2 scallions, white and
light green parts only)
½ teaspoon dried rosemary
¼ teaspoon coarsely grated lime
peel
2 tablespoons freshly squeezed
lime juice
1 tablespoon cornstarch dissolved
in ¼ cup buttermilk

Makes about 1 cup

Calories per tablespoon: 5.2
Fat per tablespoon: 0.1 g.
Cholesterol per tablespoon: 0.1 mg.

An interesting herb/citrus blend in a not-so-traditional version of white sauce.

Put chicken stock, scallion, and rosemary in saucepan. Cook over medium heat for about 3 minutes. Stir in lime peel and juice. Whisk in cornstarch/buttermilk mixture. Continue to cook, whisking constantly, until sauce has thickened (about 2 minutes). Serve immediately.

Suggested pairings: grilled or broiled fish or chicken

This sauce may be stored in the refrigerator for up to two days.

DILL SAUCE

1 cup skim milk
1 tablespoon instant nonfat dry
    milk powder
1 tablespoon cornstarch
⅛ teaspoon salt
⅛ teaspoon white pepper
1 tablespoon freshly squeezed
    lemon juice
2 tablespoons chopped fresh dill
2 tablespoons finely chopped
    scallion (about 1½–2 scallions,
    white part only)

Makes about 1 cup

Calories per tablespoon: 9.1
Fat per tablespoon: 0
Cholesterol per tablespoon: 0.3 mg.

Although intended primarily to be served over warm entrees, we've found that this sauce can perk up cold fish quite nicely as well. We suggest you chop an extra teaspoon of fresh dill for garnish, which complements the flecks of dill in the sauce.

Remove 2 tablespoons of skim milk from the cup, transfer to a small bowl, and add dry milk powder and cornstarch. Mix thoroughly to a paste and set aside. Warm the rest of the milk in a small heavy-bottomed saucepan over low heat for about 4 minutes. Add the paste to the warm milk gradually, whisking constantly. Add salt and white pepper, whisking constantly over very low heat until sauce has thickened (about 2 minutes). Whisk in lemon juice, dill, and scallion. Remove pan from heat and continue to whisk for another minute. Serve immediately.

Suggested pairings: poached or grilled salmon, broiled swordfish, chicken

This sauce may be stored in the refrigerator for one day.

HORSERADISH SAUCE

1 cup skim milk
1 tablespoon instant nonfat dry
   milk powder
1 tablespoon cornstarch
2 tablespoons prepared
   horseradish

Makes about 1 cup

Calories per tablespoon: 8.9
Fat per tablespoon: 0
Cholesterol per tablespoon: 0.3 mg.

Pure white and pungent, this sauce is excellent for basting and topping beef. It works well with veggies too.

Remove 2 tablespoons of skim milk from the cup, transfer to a small bowl, and add the dry milk powder and cornstarch. Mix thoroughly to a paste and set aside. Warm the rest of the milk in a small heavy-bottomed saucepan over low heat for about 4 minutes. Whisk about a quarter of the warmed milk into the paste, then mix the paste into the pan of warm milk, whisking constantly over very low heat until thick (about 2 minutes). Whisk in horseradish. Remove pan from heat and continue to whisk for another minute. Serve immediately.

Suggested pairings: sliced roast beef, beef brisket, steamed broccoli florets, sliced zucchini

This sauce may be stored in the refrigerator for one day.

TARRAGON MUSTARD SAUCE

1 cup skim milk
2 tablespoons potato starch
⅛ teaspoon salt
⅛ teaspoon white pepper
2 teaspoons dry mustard
2 teaspoons tarragon vinegar

Makes about 1 cup

Calories per tablespoon: 11.1
Fat per tablespoon: 0.2 g.
Cholesterol per tablespoon: 0.3 mg.

This sauce provides a lively flavor boost for bland foods and has a golden tint that can perk up even the palest piece of whitefish or chicken breast.

Remove 2 tablespoons of skim milk from the cup, transfer to a small bowl, and add the potato starch. Mix thoroughly to a paste and set aside. Warm the rest of the milk in a small heavy-bottomed saucepan over low heat for about 4 minutes. Whisk about one quarter of the warmed milk into the paste to prevent lumping, then whisk the paste back into the pan of warm milk. Add salt and white pepper, whisking constantly over very low heat until thick (about 4 minutes). Whisk in dry mustard and tarragon vinegar. Serve immediately.

Suggested pairings: chicken, monkfish, sole

This sauce may be stored in the refrigerator for one day.

TARRAGON BUTTER SAUCE

1 tablespoon butter
1 tablespoon all-purpose flour
1 cup chicken stock (canned or see
    Index for recipe)
¼ cup tarragon vinegar
1 tablespoon finely chopped fresh
    tarragon or 1 teaspoon dried
    tarragon
1 teaspoon fennel seeds

Makes about 1 cup

Calories per tablespoon: 11.3
Fat per tablespoon: 0.8 g.
Cholesterol per tablespoon: 2.1 mg.

This flavorful sauce is thickened slightly with a lighter version of the classic roux, a mixture of flour and butter—but not enough to make it fattening. We prefer the taste of butter, but if you're watching your cholesterol you can substitute margarine or a margarine/butter blend.

Warm butter in a small heavy-bottomed saucepan over medium heat just until melted and foamy. Whisk in flour. Cook 2 to 3 minutes until mixture is a light tan, whisking constantly (be careful not to let it burn or stick). Whisk in chicken stock and vinegar. Whisking constantly, bring to a boil over medium heat and continue to boil until thickened (about 30 seconds). Remove pan from heat and whisk in tarragon and fennel seeds. Serve immediately.

Suggested pairings: chicken, shrimp, cod, steamed vegetables

This sauce may be stored in the refrigerator for up to three days, and in the freezer for up to one month.

BASIL BUTTER SAUCE

1 tablespoon butter
1 tablespoon all-purpose flour
1 cup chicken stock (canned or see
    Index for recipe)
¼ cup balsamic vinegar
1 tablespoon finely chopped fresh
    basil
1 tablespoon tomato paste

Makes about 1¼ cups

Calories per tablespoon: 9.1
Fat per tablespoon: 0.7 g.
Cholesterol per tablespoon: 1.7 mg.

You might want to try this sauce over spaghetti squash, sprinkled with a bit of parmesan cheese or a few pine nuts. It's a much lighter version of pasta with pesto sauce.

Warm butter in a small heavy-bottomed saucepan over medium heat just until melted and foamy. Whisk in flour. Cook 2 to 3 minutes until mixture is a light tan, whisking constantly (be careful not to let it burn or stick). Whisk in chicken stock and vinegar. Bring to a boil over medium heat, whisking constantly. Whisk in basil. Continuing to whisk, boil until thickened (about 30 seconds). Turn heat down to low and whisk in tomato paste. Return just to a boil. Serve immediately.

Suggested pairings: chicken, veal, pork

This sauce may be stored in the refrigerator for up to three days, and in the freezer for up to one month.

GARLIC MUSTARD SAUCE

¼ cup chicken stock (canned or see
    Index for recipe)
¼ cup white wine vinegar
2 teaspoons finely minced white
    onion
2 cloves garlic
1 tablespoon Dijon-style mustard
½ tablespoon butter

Makes about ½ cup

Calories per tablespoon: 11.7
Fat per tablespoon: 0.9 g.
Cholesterol per tablespoon: 2.1 mg.

This pleasantly tangy concoction can do triple duty for basting, dipping, and topping. A favorite hors d'oeuvre is prepared by skewering Canadian bacon and basting with garlic mustard sauce before cooking on the grill. The sauce can then be used for dipping.

Bring stock, vinegar, and onion to a boil in a saucepan over medium heat. Simmer uncovered over medium-low heat for 5 minutes. Crush in garlic, using a garlic press. Whisk in mustard. Heat another 2 to 3 minutes. Swirl in butter. Serve immediately.

Suggested pairings: chicken, sole, swordfish, shrimp, smoked meat

This sauce may be stored in the refrigerator for up to three days, or up to one month in the freezer.

CURRY SAUCE

1 teaspoon canola oil
1 tablespoon chopped white onion
1 teaspoon curry powder
½ cup beef stock (canned or see
    Index for recipe)

Makes about ½ cup

Calories per tablespoon: 7.3
Fat per tablespoon: 0.7 g.
Cholesterol per tablespoon: 0

We prefer the subtle elegance of mild imported Indian curry powder, but let the limits of your taste buds dictate—the hotter the curry powder, the hotter the sauce. In addition to its role as an escort to main courses and vegetables, this sauce is quite good with flaked crab as an appetizer.

Heat oil for about 30 seconds in a small heavy-bottomed saucepan over medium heat. Add onion and sauté until golden (about 3 minutes), taking care not to let it brown or burn. Stir in curry powder until well blended (onion is coated). Whisk in stock. Bring to a boil over medium heat. Turn heat down to low and simmer uncovered for 3 minutes. Serve immediately.

Suggested pairings: steamed vegetables, cod, monkfish, chicken

This sauce may be stored in the refrigerator for up to five days, or in the freezer for up to three months.

CREAMY CURRY SAUCE

1 tablespoon butter
1 tablespoon all-purpose flour
1 cup chicken stock (canned or see
    Index for recipe)
⅛ cup white wine vinegar
2 teaspoons finely diced white
    onion
1½ teaspoons curry powder

Makes about 1⅛ cups

Calories per tablespoon: 9.8
Fat per tablespoon: 0.7 g.
Cholesterol per tablespoon: 1.8 mg.

In addition to being a flavorful sauce, this is also an excellent base for stews.

Warm butter in a small heavy-bottomed saucepan over medium heat just until melted and foamy. Whisk in flour. Cook about 5 minutes until mixture is a rich dark brown, whisking constantly (be careful not to let it burn or stick). Whisk in chicken stock and vinegar. Bring to a boil over medium heat, whisking constantly. Whisk in onion and curry powder. Continuing to whisk, boil until thickened (about 30 seconds). Remove from heat and continue to whisk for an additional 30 seconds. Serve immediately.

Suggested pairings: lamb, shrimp, chicken, vegetables, baked potato

This sauce may be stored in the refrigerator for up to two days, or up to one month in the freezer.

SPICY DIPPING SAUCE

½ cup chicken stock (canned or see
    Index for recipe)
2 tablespoons red wine vinegar
¼ cup soy sauce
⅛ teaspoon chili paste with garlic
2 teaspoons cornstarch dissolved
    in 2 teaspoons water

Makes about ¾ cup

Calories per tablespoon: 9.5
Fat per tablespoon: 0.3 g.
Cholesterol per tablespoon: 0

This flavorful sauce serves up a hint of the Orient, with a hit of spice for extra interest.

In a small saucepan over medium heat, combine stock, vinegar, soy sauce, and chili paste. Bring to a boil. Whisk in cornstarch mixture. Turn heat down to low and simmer until thick (about 2 minutes), stirring constantly. Serve immediately.

Suggested pairings: shrimp, scallops, chicken, wontons, beef satay

This sauce may be stored in the refrigerator for up to five days, or in the freezer for up to six months.

WASABI SAUCE

2 teaspoons wasabi powder
(Japanese horseradish powder)
1 teaspoon soy sauce
1 teaspoon water
1½ tablespoons finely diced
scallion (about 1 scallion, white
and light green parts only)
1½ teaspoons finely minced garlic
(about 2 cloves)
½ teaspoon raw sesame seeds
¾ cup chicken stock (canned or see
Index for recipe)
2 teaspoons cornstarch dissolved
in 1 tablespoon water

Makes about ¾ cup

Calories per tablespoon: 5.1
Fat per tablespoon: 0.1 g.
Cholesterol per tablespoon: 0

The inspiration for this recipe is wasabi butter, with which we grill fish. Although here in a much leaner incarnation, the powerful flavor of the Japanese horseradish powder still comes ringing through.

Dissolve wasabi powder in soy sauce and water, mixing to a paste. Set aside for 5 to 10 minutes. Put scallion, garlic, sesame seeds, and chicken stock in a saucepan and bring to a boil over medium heat. Reduce heat to low and whisk in wasabi mixture, taking care to dissolve thoroughly. Whisk in cornstarch mixture. Cook, whisking constantly, until slightly thickened (about 1 minute). Let cool. Serve at room temperature.

Suggested pairings: broiled or grilled tuna or salmon, baked potato, steamed white or brown rice

This sauce may be stored in the refrigerator for up to three days, or in the freezer for up to six months.

4
SAVORY FRUIT-FLAVORED SAUCES

SAVORY RASPBERRY SAUCE
CITRUS SAUCE
CRANBERRY ORANGE SAUCE
BLACK CHERRY SAUCE
SPICY APRICOT SAUCE
CRUNCHY GINGER SAUCE
SWEET & SOUR POLYNESIAN SAUCE
ORANGE RAISIN SAUCE
RAISIN FIG SAUCE
BANANA KIWI PUREE

SAVORY RASPBERRY SAUCE

¾ cup whole raspberries (fresh or
    unsweetened frozen)
⅓ cup finely minced white onion
    (about ⅓ medium onion)
3 tablespoons raspberry vinegar
⅓ cup chicken stock (canned or see
    Index for recipe)
Pinch of black pepper

Makes about 1¼ cups

Calories per tablespoon: 3.8
Fat per tablespoon: 0
Cholesterol per tablespoon: 0

A flavorful raspberry puree adds intensity to this sauce, while whole raspberries lend a touch of style. It's particularly delightful with pheasant or other game.

Puree ½ cup of the raspberries to a smooth consistency in a food processor or blender and set aside. Place onion and vinegar in a saucepan and bring to a boil over medium heat. Continue to boil until liquid in pan is reduced by half (3 to 4 minutes). Whisk in chicken stock and pepper and return to boil. Whisk in raspberry puree and return to boil. Continue to boil over medium heat for 1 minute. Add remaining ¼ cup whole raspberries and cook 1 additional minute. Serve immediately.

Suggested pairings: pork roast, chicken, cornish hens, game birds

This sauce may be stored in the refrigerator for up to five days, or in the freezer for up to three months.

CITRUS SAUCE

½ cup grapefruit juice (fresh, if possible)

¼ cup orange juice (fresh, if possible)

1 teaspoon potato starch dissolved in 1 tablespoon freshly squeezed lemon juice

½ cup fresh grapefruit segments

Makes about 1⅓ cups

Calories per tablespoon: 6.3
Fat per tablespoon: 0
Cholesterol per tablespoon: 0

Conceived as a sauce for entrees, it is also wonderful as an accompaniment for broiled bananas as a dessert.

Warm grapefruit juice and orange juice for 3 minutes in an uncovered saucepan over low heat. Whisk in potato starch mixture (be careful not to let it boil). Continue to cook, whisking constantly, for 2 minutes. Add grapefruit segments (stir in gently, being careful not to break up grapefruit). Serve immediately.

Suggested pairings: tuna, swordfish, chicken, baked ham

This sauce may be stored in the refrigerator for up to five days.

CRANBERRY ORANGE SAUCE

½ cup orange juice (fresh, if possible)
2 cups cranberries (slightly less than 1 12-ounce package)
1 cup peeled, seeded, and chopped navel orange (about 1 large orange)
⅛ teaspoon ground cinnamon
⅛ teaspoon ground allspice
⅛ teaspoon ground nutmeg
⅛ teaspoon sugar

Makes about 2 cups

Calories per tablespoon: 6.8
Fat per tablespoon: 0
Cholesterol per tablespoon: 0

Not just for Thanksgiving, this sauce can accompany a hen just off the grill as smartly as the holiday turkey. Buy cranberries in the fall, when they're readily available and inexpensive, and freeze for year-round use. If you're using frozen berries in this recipe, there's no need to thaw them first—just add them, frozen, to the mixture in the saucepan.

Combine orange juice, cranberries, and orange in a saucepan. Mix well, and bring to a boil over medium heat. Boil 5 minutes. Add cinnamon, allspice, nutmeg, and sugar, turn heat down to low, and simmer uncovered for about 15 minutes. If you are using fresh cranberries, the skins may split when cooked, releasing the fruit; if berries have been frozen, you'll need to mash some with the side of a wooden spoon while simmering. Do not overcook. Serve at room temperature or chilled (cover if chilling).

Suggested pairings: pork, game birds, turkey, grilled chicken or cornish hens

This sauce may be stored in the refrigerator for up to 10 days.

BLACK CHERRY SAUCE

1½ cups pitted whole dark sweet
    cherries (fresh or unsweetened
    frozen)
¼ cup warm water
1 tablespoon port wine
Pinch of black pepper

Makes about 1½ cups

Calories per tablespoon: 8.9
Fat per tablespoon: 0.1 g.
Cholesterol per tablespoon: 0

If you're using frozen cherries, don't confuse the type of cherry called for in the recipe (sweet cherries, as opposed to the sour variety), with the way they're packed (you want cherries that are packed unsweetened, that is, with no sugar added).

Put ¾ cup of the cherries in the bowl of a food processor or blender. While adding warm water through the feed tube, puree to a smooth consistency. Transfer puree to a small saucepan and bring to a boil over medium heat. Whisk in port wine and black pepper and return to a boil. Continue to boil until slightly thickened (about 2 minutes). Whisk in remaining ¾ cup whole cherries and return just to a boil. Serve immediately.

Suggested pairings: cornish hens, roasted chicken, pheasant, duck

This sauce may be stored in the refrigerator for up to five days, or in the freezer for up to three months.

SPICY APRICOT SAUCE

¾ cup apricot nectar
⅓ cup balsamic vinegar
¼ cup apricot spreadable fruit
1 tablespoon soy sauce
⅛ teaspoon crushed red pepper
½ tablespoon raw sesame seeds

Makes about 1⅓ cups

Calories per tablespoon: 15.9
Fat per tablespoon: 0.1 g.
Cholesterol per tablespoon: 0

This goes quite nicely with finger food, as well as a topping for main courses.

Combine nectar and vinegar in a heavy-bottomed saucepan, stir, and bring to a low boil over medium heat. Stir in spreadable fruit and return to a boil. Add soy sauce, crushed pepper, and sesame seeds. Return to a boil over medium heat and let cook for 1 additional minute. Serve immediately.

Suggested pairings: chicken, shrimp, scrod, wontons

This sauce may be stored in the refrigerator for up to five days, or in the freezer for up to four months.

CRUNCHY GINGER SAUCE

1 tablespoon finely chopped
  candied ginger
1 tablespoon orange juice (fresh, if
  possible)
⅛ teaspoon finely grated orange
  peel
½ cup plain nonfat yogurt

Makes about ½ cup

Calories per tablespoon: 12.6
Fat per tablespoon: 0
Cholesterol per tablespoon: 0.3 mg.

Those who love ginger as much as we do will want to use this recipe in as many ways as possible. In addition to serving this sauce atop entrees and vegetables, use it chilled as a marinade or as a dressing for fresh fruit. The ginger taste intensifies if the sauce is refrigerated.

Place ginger and orange juice in a bowl and stir well. Add peel and yogurt. Mix all ingredients together thoroughly. Serve at room temperature or chilled (cover if chilling).

Suggested pairings: chicken, steamed string beans, broccoli, snow peas

This sauce may be stored in the refrigerator for up to two days (if within freshness guidelines for yogurt; check expiration date on carton).

SWEET & SOUR POLYNESIAN SAUCE

½ cup canned crushed pineapple
  packed in natural unsweetened
  juice, drained
½ cup orange juice (fresh, if
  possible)
1 teaspoon finely chopped orange
  peel
¼ teaspoon ground nutmeg
⅛ teaspoon black pepper
¼ teaspoon grated fresh ginger
1 tablespoon freshly squeezed
  lemon juice
2 tablespoons white vinegar
1 teaspoon soy sauce
2 tablespoons honey
2 teaspoons cornstarch dissolved
  in 1 tablespoon water

Makes about 1½ cups

Calories per tablespoon: 12.1
Fat per tablespoon: 0
Cholesterol per tablespoon: 0

This sauce conjures up a South Seas feel faster than the decor at Trader Vic's. The recipe calls for freshly grated ginger, which some cooks use infrequently. To keep ginger fresh between uses, store ginger root in a resealable plastic bag in the freezer. Just take out and grate when needed.

Heat pineapple and orange juice in an uncovered saucepan over low heat for 2 to 3 minutes. Add peel, nutmeg, black pepper, and ginger, mixing in thoroughly. Stir in lemon juice, vinegar, and soy sauce. Turn heat up to medium and cook another minute. Whisk in honey. Bring to a boil over medium heat and boil for 1 minute. Whisk in cornstarch mixture and bring back to a boil. Continue to cook until thick (about 30 seconds), whisking constantly. Serve immediately.

Suggested pairings: chicken, pork roast, ribs

This sauce may be stored in the refrigerator for up to five days, or in the freezer for up to three months.

ORANGE RAISIN SAUCE

½ cup seedless raisins (any variety)
½ cup boiling water
1 tablespoon cornstarch dissolved in 1 tablespoon sweetened white grape juice concentrate (undiluted)
1 cup orange juice (fresh, if possible)
⅛ teaspoon black pepper
1 teaspoon freshly squeezed lemon juice

Makes about 1½ cups

Calories per tablespoon: 16.6
Fat per tablespoon: 0
Cholesterol per tablespoon: 0

A rich, indulgent sauce, this is reminiscent of the sweet raisin sauces that always topped the ham at special family gatherings.

Place raisins in a bowl and cover with boiling water. Let soak about 5 minutes, until plump. Drain and set aside. Bring cornstarch/juice concentrate mixture and orange juice to a boil in a small saucepan over medium heat, stirring occasionally. Stir in pepper and lemon juice. Return to a boil. Add raisins. Serve immediately.

Suggested pairings: pork, ham, roast tongue, game birds

This sauce may be stored in the refrigerator for up to five days, or in the freezer for up to three months.

RAISIN FIG SAUCE

4 dried figs (preferably Black Mission), chopped
2 tablespoons seedless raisins (any variety)
⅛ teaspoon ground cloves
1 cup water
1 teaspoon cornstarch dissolved in ½ tablespoon water
⅛ teaspoon black pepper
1 tablespoon freshly squeezed lemon juice
1 tablespoon white vinegar

Makes about 1⅓ cups

Calories per tablespoon: 12.4
Fat per tablespoon: 0.1 g.
Cholesterol per tablespoon: 0

Part sauce, part relish, with a hint of sweet and sour flavor underlying the distinctive taste of fig.

Place figs, raisins, ground cloves, and water in a heavy-bottomed saucepan. Heat for 10 minutes, uncovered, over medium-low heat. Whisk in cornstarch mixture and cook for about 3 minutes. Whisk in pepper, lemon juice, and vinegar. Cook for 2 minutes more. Serve immediately.

Suggested pairings: chicken, pork roast, baked ham, roast tongue, game birds

This sauce may be stored in the refrigerator for up to three days.

BANANA KIWI PUREE

1 very ripe banana
1 kiwi
½ teaspoon freshly squeezed lemon
   juice
⅛ teaspoon black pepper
½ cup chicken stock (canned or see
   Index for recipe)
¼ cup white wine vinegar
2 teaspoons finely minced white
   onion

Makes about 1½ cups

Calories per tablespoon: 7.2
Fat per tablespoon: 0
Cholesterol per tablespoon: 0

The distinct but somewhat elusive flavor of this sauce will keep your guests guessing as to the ingredients. It also works well for basting.

Peel and cut banana into four chunks. Peel kiwi and cut into quarters. Put banana and kiwi in the bowl of a food processor or a blender and add lemon juice and black pepper. Puree and set aside. In a saucepan over medium heat, bring stock, vinegar, and onion to a boil. Simmer uncovered for 5 minutes over medium-low heat. Remove from heat and whisk in puree. Return to heat and warm for 1 to 2 minutes over medium-low heat. Serve immediately.

Suggested pairings: whitefish, scrod, broiled chicken

This sauce is quite perishable and should be used immediately.

5
VEGETABLE-FLAVORED SAUCES

ROASTED RED PEPPER SAUCE
GREEN CHILI COULIS
CHUNKY LEEK PUREE
AVOCADO PUREE
FENNEL PUREE
ANCHOVY OLIVE SAUCE
CLASSIC MUSHROOM SAUCE
WHITE MUSHROOM SAUCE
ORANGE BEET SAUCE
BLACK BEAN SAUCE

ROASTED RED PEPPER SAUCE

1 small red bell pepper, sliced in
  half lengthwise and seeded
¼ cup chicken stock (canned or see
  Index for recipe)
½ cup coarsely chopped white
  onion (about ½ medium onion)
3 cloves garlic
½ tablespoon red wine vinegar
1 well-packed tablespoon chopped
  fresh basil

Makes about ⅔ cup

Calories per tablespoon: 6.4
Fat per tablespoon: 0.1 g.
Cholesterol per tablespoon: 0

Don't be intimidated by the added step of roasting the pepper in this recipe. It's really quick and easy if you follow the simple steps below. The sauce is robust, versatile, and well worth the small effort.

Broil pepper until charred (about 5 minutes on each side). Remove from broiler and set aside to cool. Put chicken stock and onion in a saucepan and bring to a boil over medium heat. Crush in garlic, using a garlic press. Continue boiling until almost all liquid in the pan is evaporated (3 to 5 minutes) and remove from heat. Once pepper is cool enough to handle, peel off the charred skin. Combine pepper, onion, and garlic in the bowl of a food processor or a blender. Add vinegar and basil. Puree to a smooth consistency. Serve immediately.

Suggested pairings: turkey breast, chicken, monkfish, cod, veal chop

This sauce may be stored in the refrigerator for up to five days, or in the freezer for up to one month.

GREEN CHILI COULIS

3 poblano chili peppers
1 small jalapeño pepper
1 medium white onion, cut into
    eighths
1 tablespoon canola oil
½ cup chicken stock (canned or see
    Index for recipe)
1 tablespoon freshly squeezed
    lemon juice

Makes about 1¼ cups

Calories per tablespoon: 12.5
Fat per tablespoon: 0.8 g.
Cholesterol per tablespoon: 0

This chunky sauce is quite hot to begin with, and gets even zippier if it sits in the refrigerator for a few days. Be sure to carefully follow the directions noted below when working with the peppers called for in this recipe.

Wearing rubber gloves, remove the stems from the chilies and cut each pod in half lengthwise. Remove all seeds and veins from inside. Hold pods under cold running water to be sure they are free of seeds. Follow the same procedure for the jalapeño pepper. Place chili peppers, jalapeño pepper, and onion in the bowl of a food processor or blender and chop to a chunky consistency (similar to that of pickle relish). Chopping also can be done by hand, using a wooden bowl and a metal chopper, or on a cutting board, using a large chef's knife.

Heat oil for about 30 seconds in a nonstick frying pan over high heat. Add mixture from bowl and sauté, stirring constantly, until no liquid remains in the pan (2 to 3 minutes). Add chicken stock, lower to medium heat, stir, and bring back to a strong boil. Stir in lemon juice. Serve immediately.

Suggested pairings: pork chops, sole, red snapper, broiled tomatoes

This sauce may be stored in the refrigerator for up to five days.

CHUNKY LEEK PUREE

2 cups cleaned and chopped leeks
    (2–3 large leeks or about 6
    baby leeks, white and light
    green parts only)
1 cup chicken stock (canned or see
    Index for recipe)
⅛ teaspoon ground nutmeg
Pinch of cayenne pepper (up to ⅛
    teaspoon, to taste)
2 tablespoons evaporated skim
    milk

Makes about 1 cup

Calories per tablespoon: 11.0
Fat per tablespoon: 0.1 g.
Cholesterol per tablespoon: 0.1 mg.

To clean leeks, chop off the root end and peel and discard the outer layer. Pull the underlying layers back, and rinse thoroughly under cold running water. Slice lengthwise from the bulbous white end to the beginning of the green tail. Fan open and rinse thoroughly.

Place leeks and chicken stock in a saucepan. Bring to a boil over medium heat. Continue to boil for 2 minutes. Turn heat down to low and simmer uncovered for 20 minutes. Remove from heat. Leaving cooking liquid in pan, transfer leeks to a bowl and mash well with a fork. Return mashed leeks to the pan, and whisk into cooking liquid over low heat. Whisk in nutmeg and cayenne pepper, then evaporated skim milk. Turn heat up to medium and return to a boil, whisking constantly. Serve immediately.

Suggested pairings: poached salmon, roast pork, steamed asparagus or cauliflower

This sauce may be stored in the refrigerator for up to three days.

AVOCADO PUREE

½ cup chicken stock (canned or see Index for recipe)
2 tablespoons white wine vinegar
2 teaspoons finely chopped white onion
⅛ teaspoon hot sauce
1 ripe avocado, peeled and pitted

Makes about 1½ cups

Calories per tablespoon: 13.4
Fat per tablespoon: 1 3 g.
Cholesterol per tablespoon: 0

This smooth, tangy sauce derives its distinct and buttery taste from the nutritious avocado. It's particularly good at perking up broiled or grilled white fish or chicken.

Put chicken stock, vinegar, and onion in a saucepan and bring to a boil over medium heat. Reduce heat to medium-low and simmer uncovered for 5 minutes. Stir in hot sauce. Remove pan from heat.

Puree avocado to a smooth consistency in a food processor (or mash in a bowl using a fork). Slowly drizzle chicken stock mixture into avocado through the feed tube of the food processor, processing constantly (or drizzle into the bowl, whisking constantly, if avocado was mashed by hand). Serve at room temperature.

Suggested pairings: monkfish, sole, chicken

This sauce is quite perishable and should be used immediately.

FENNEL PUREE

2 cups chopped fennel (about 1
    medium fennel bulb, white part
    only)
½ cup water
½ cup chicken stock (canned or see
    Index for recipe)
⅛ teaspoon white pepper
1 tablespoon evaporated skim milk

Makes about 1 cup

Calories per tablespoon: 9.5
Fat per tablespoon: 0.1 g.
Cholesterol per tablespoon: 0

A creamy sauce with a unique licorice flavor that also works well with appetizers—it's great spooned warm over baked clams or oysters.

Put fennel and water in a saucepan and bring to a boil over medium heat. Cover and simmer for about 10 minutes, until fennel is soft and easily mashed with a fork. Transfer fennel and cooking liquid to the bowl of a food processor or blender. Add chicken stock, pepper, and evaporated skim milk. Puree to a smooth consistency. Serve immediately.

Suggested pairings: pork, veal, duck

This sauce may be stored in the refrigerator for up to three days.

ANCHOVY OLIVE SAUCE

1 anchovy fillet (canned)
1 cup chopped black olives
1 tablespoon Worcestershire sauce
½ cup plain nonfat yogurt
1 tablespoon minced garlic (about
    4 cloves)
1 tablespoon dried basil

Makes about 2 cups

Calories per tablespoon: 6.6
Fat per tablespoon: 0
Cholesterol per tablespoon: 0.1 mg.

There's no middle ground when it comes to anchovies—you either love them or avoid them. For those who fall into the former category, this thick sauce should prove a treat spooned over entrees, side dishes, or shrimp served as an appetizer.

Chop and mash anchovy fillet. Mix in a bowl with olives and Worcestershire sauce. Blend in yogurt, then garlic and basil. Mix thoroughly. Serve at room temperature.

Suggested pairings: whitefish, shrimp, grilled vegetables

This sauce may be stored in the refrigerator for up to three days (within freshness guidelines for yogurt; check expiration date on carton).

CLASSIC MUSHROOM SAUCE

4 cups (about 1 pound) finely
    chopped fresh mushrooms
½ tablespoon freshly squeezed
    lemon juice
¼ cup water
1 cup beef stock (canned or see
    Index for recipe)
1 tablespoon cornstarch dissolved
    in 1 tablespoon water
1 teaspoon soy sauce
¼ teaspoon nutmeg
⅛ teaspoon black pepper

Makes about 1½ cups

Calories per tablespoon: 5.3
Fat per tablespoon: 0.1 g.
Cholesterol per tablespoon: 0

Our version of the classic brown sauce—much lower in calories, but just as versatile.

Simmer mushrooms, lemon juice, and water in an uncovered saucepan over low heat for 20 minutes. Whisk in beef stock, cornstarch mixture, soy sauce, and spices. Cook about 1 minute more until thick, whisking constantly. Serve immediately.

Suggested pairings: roast beef, steak, veal, turkey, broiled tuna, baked or mashed potatoes

This sauce may be stored in the refrigerator for up to five days.

WHITE MUSHROOM SAUCE

4 cups (about 1 pound) finely
  chopped fresh mushrooms
½ tablespoon freshly squeezed
  lemon juice
¼ cup water
⅛ teaspoon white pepper
¼ teaspoon dried thyme
¼ cup evaporated skim milk
½ cup buttermilk
⅛ teaspoon sugar
½ teaspoon cornstarch dissolved in
  1 teaspoon water

Makes about 1¾ cups

Calories per tablespoon: 6.5
Fat per tablespoon: 0.1 g.
Cholesterol per tablespoon: 0.2 mg.

Mushrooms contain an enormous amount of water, so don't worry that you are simmering in very little liquid. You'll be surprised just how much water they generate, which then has to be boiled off.

Simmer mushrooms, lemon juice, and water in an uncovered saucepan over low heat for 20 minutes, stirring occasionally. Turn heat up to medium and boil until most of the water in the pan has evaporated (5 to 10 minutes). Whisk in white pepper and thyme. Whisk in evaporated skim milk. Slowly whisk in buttermilk, a little at a time. Whisk in sugar, then cornstarch mixture. Bring back to a boil, whisking constantly. Remove from heat and serve immediately.

Suggested pairings: chicken, steamed vegetables, sliced boiled potatoes

This sauce may be stored in the refrigerator for up to three days.

ORANGE BEET SAUCE

1 4½-ounce jar pure strained infant-food beets (no sugar or starch added)
¼ cup orange juice (fresh, if possible)
⅛ teaspoon ground cloves
¼ teaspoon tarragon vinegar

Makes about ¾ cup

Calories per tablespoon: 8.9
Fat per tablespoon: 0
Cholesterol per tablespoon: 0

We use strained infant-food beets in this recipe to avoid the mess of boiling beets, which can leave both the cook and the kitchen a distinct shade of red. You may want to experiment with the use of other pure, strained infant-food fruits and vegetables, which can be real time-savers.

Place strained beets in saucepan over low heat. Whisk in orange juice and cloves. Then whisk in tarragon vinegar. Continue to heat, whisking constantly, for about 2 minutes. Serve immediately.

Suggested pairings: pork, sliced turkey breast, steamed cabbage (top with celery seeds or caraway seeds)

This sauce may be stored in the refrigerator for up to three days.

BLACK BEAN SAUCE

1 tablespoon canola oil
1 tablespoon minced garlic (3–4
    cloves)
3 tablespoons minced scallion
    (about 2 scallions, white and
    light green parts only)
½ cup canned black beans, drained
    and rinsed under cold water
½ teaspoon grated fresh ginger
⅛ teaspoon crushed red pepper
1 tablespoon soy sauce
½ cup chicken stock (canned or see
    Index for recipe)
½ tablespoon cornstarch dissolved
    in 1 tablespoon water

Makes about 1 cup

Calories per tablespoon: 17.8
Fat per tablespoon: 0.9 g.
Cholesterol per tablespoon: 0

This sauce comes in a bit above the average calorie count of our other sauces, but black beans are so healthful and high in protein that this qualifies as a virtuous indulgence.

In a heavy-bottomed saucepan, heat oil for about 30 seconds over medium heat. Add garlic and scallions. Sauté for 1 minute, taking care not to brown scallions. Add beans and mix them in, then add ginger and red pepper. Sauté for an additional 30 seconds. Add soy sauce and chicken stock. Bring to a boil over medium heat. Stir in cornstarch mixture until sauce thickens. Serve immediately.

Suggested pairings: chicken, pork, shrimp

This sauce may be stored in the refrigerator for up to five days.

6
DRESSINGS

ALMOST NO-CAL DRESSING
POPPY SEED DRESSING
MANGO BASIL DRESSING
CREAMY TARRAGON DRESSING
CANTALOUPE YOGURT DRESSING
CUCUMBER YOGURT DRESSING
DILL YOGURT DRESSING
MINT YOGURT DRESSING
LEMON YOGURT DRESSING
RED WINE VINEGAR DRESSING
MUSTARD VINAIGRETTE

ALMOST NO-CAL DRESSING

½ cup white wine vinegar
1 clove garlic
¼ teaspoon dried oregano
1 teaspoon finely chopped fresh
   cilantro
¼ teaspoon freshly squeezed lemon
   juice

Makes about ½ cup

Calories per tablespoon: 2.8
Fat per tablespoon: 0
Cholesterol per tablespoon: 0

The ultimate svelte dressing—no fat or cholesterol, almost no calories, and bursting with fresh herb flavor and aroma. Chop cilantro in the food processor for a finer consistency, by hand for coarser consistency. The longer the dressing sits in the refrigerator, the more pronounced the cilantro taste becomes. For variety, try substituting fresh tarragon or basil for cilantro (calories may vary slightly). This recipe can easily be cut in half or doubled.

Using a garlic press, crush the garlic into the vinegar. Mix in oregano, cilantro, and lemon juice, and shake or whisk vigorously. Cover and chill for the flavors to blend together.

Suggested pairings: green salads, sliced tomatoes, cold fish, sliced cold chicken breast

This dressing may be stored in the refrigerator for up to three days.

POPPY SEED DRESSING

¾ cup plain nonfat yogurt
3 tablespoons tarragon vinegar
1 teaspoon grated onion
½ teaspoon dry mustard
1½ teaspoons freshly squeezed
    lemon juice
1 teaspoon dark brown sugar
1 teaspoon poppy seeds

Makes about 1 cup

Calories per tablespoon: 8.6
Fat per tablespoon: 0.1 g.
Cholesterol per tablespoon: 0.2 mg.

A special favorite of ours, this dressing is as tangy as it is cool and refreshing.

Place yogurt in a bowl. Add remaining ingredients, one at a time, in order listed, mixing each in well. Cover and chill. Serve chilled.

Suggested pairings: green salads, sliced chilled cantaloupe or honeydew melon

This dressing may be stored in the refrigerator for up to three days (within freshness guidelines for yogurt; check expiration date on carton).

MANGO BASIL DRESSING

¼ cup mango nectar
¼ cup white wine vinegar
½ tablespoon chopped fresh basil
   or ½ teaspoon dried basil
¼ teaspoon dry mustard
⅛ teaspoon freshly ground black
   pepper

Makes about ½ cup

Calories per tablespoon: 5.8
Fat per tablespoon: 0
Cholesterol per tablespoon: 0

In addition to dressing up salads, this mixture also goes quite well with roasted chicken. Use it to baste and top the chicken, and garnish with slices of zucchini or cucumber.

Combine all ingredients in a bowl or a jar and mix or shake thoroughly. Serve at room temperature.

Suggested pairings: green salads with ham, smoked turkey, or diced chicken breast

This dressing may be stored in the refrigerator for up to three days.

CREAMY TARRAGON DRESSING

¼ cup buttermilk
½ tablespoon tarragon vinegar
¼ teaspoon dry mustard
Pinch of salt (up to ⅛ teaspoon, to taste)
⅛ teaspoon freshly ground black pepper
⅛ teaspoon dried tarragon
¼ teaspoon chopped fresh chives

Makes about ¼ cup

Calories per tablespoon: 7.4
Fat per tablespoon: 0.2 g.
Cholesterol per tablespoon: 0.6 mg.

Fresh and elegant taste with the ease of prepackaged—you can prepare this dressing by combining the ingredients in a bottle and shaking vigorously.

Combine all ingredients in a bowl or a jar and mix or shake thoroughly. Serve at room temperature or chilled (cover if chilling).

Suggested pairings: green salads, cold steamed vegetables, sliced bell pepper, shredded carrot

This dressing may be stored in the refrigerator for up to three days.

CANTALOUPE YOGURT DRESSING

1 cup seeded and diced cantaloupe
(about ¼ small cantaloupe)
1 tablespoon freshly squeezed
lemon juice
¼ cup diced celery (about 1
medium stalk)
⅓ cup plain nonfat yogurt

Makes about 1 cup

Calories per tablespoon: 6.8
Fat per tablespoon: 0
Cholesterol per tablespoon: 0.1 mg.

A summertime dressing that's a perfect accompaniment for summer foods. It's great on a salad topped with mandarin oranges.

Place cantaloupe, lemon juice, and celery in a food processor or a blender. Puree to a smooth consistency. Transfer to a bowl and whisk in yogurt. Cover and chill. Serve chilled.

Suggested pairings: fruit salads, vegetable salads, green salads, cold turkey or tuna

This dressing may be stored in the refrigerator for up to three days (within freshness guidelines for yogurt; check expiration date on carton).

CUCUMBER YOGURT DRESSING

1 cup peeled and diced cucumber
   (about ⅓–½ cucumber)
2 tablespoons freshly squeezed
   lemon juice
¼ cup diced white onion (about ¼
   medium onion)
¼ cup diced celery (about 1
   medium stalk)
⅔ cup plain nonfat yogurt

Makes about 1⅓ cups

Calories per tablespoon: 5.9
Fat per tablespoon: 0
Cholesterol per tablespoon: 0.1 mg.

This particularly cool and refreshing dressing works well with celery stalks, radishes, and carrot sticks for a healthy appetizer or snack.

Place cucumber, lemon juice, onion, and celery in a food processor or a blender. Puree to a slightly chunky consistency. Transfer to a bowl and whisk in yogurt. Cover and chill. Serve chilled.

Suggested pairings: fruit salads, chicken salad, vegetable salads

This dressing may be stored in the refrigerator for up to three days (within freshness guidelines for yogurt; check expiration date on carton).

DILL YOGURT DRESSING

½ cup plain nonfat yogurt
¼ cup buttermilk
2 tablespoons chopped fresh dill
¼ teaspoon freshly ground black
    pepper
½ tablespoon white wine vinegar

Makes about ¾ cup

Calories per tablespoon: 8.1
Fat per tablespoon: 0.1 g.
Cholesterol per tablespoon: 0.4 mg.

This refreshing and tangy dressing is best paired with cold vegetables and meats.

In a bowl, mix all ingredients together. Cover and chill. Serve chilled.

Suggested pairings: green salads, sliced cucumbers, radishes, cold sliced chicken or turkey breast.

This dressing may be stored in the refrigerator for up to three days (within freshness guidelines for yogurt; check expiration date on carton).

MINT YOGURT DRESSING

1 cup plain nonfat yogurt
¼ cup chopped fresh mint
2 tablespoons freshly squeezed
    lemon juice

Makes about 1 cup

Calories per tablespoon: 8.6
Fat per tablespoon: 0
Cholesterol per tablespoon: 0.3 mg.

A refreshing but full-bodied accompaniment for fruit and vegetables.

In a bowl, thoroughly mix all ingredients together. Cover and chill. Serve chilled.

Suggested pairings: fruit salads, sliced fruit, cantaloupe, green salads

This dressing may be stored in the refrigerator for up to three days (within freshness guidelines for yogurt; check expiration date on carton).

LEMON YOGURT DRESSING

1 cup plain nonfat yogurt
1 tablespoon freshly squeezed
   lemon juice
1 tablespoon white wine vinegar
2 tablespoons grated onion (less
   than ¼ small onion)
¼ cup finely chopped scallion
   (about 2–3 scallions, white and
   light green parts only)
1 tablespoon chopped fresh
   cilantro
⅛ teaspoon freshly ground black
   pepper

Chopped scallion and grated white onion add a kick and a crunch to this satisfying dressing, which can also double as a marinade for chicken or fish (marinate, then baste when grilling or broiling).

Place all ingredients in a bowl and thoroughly mix together.

Suggested pairings: cold fish, chicken, or vegetables

This dressing may be stored in the refrigerator for up to three days (within freshness guidelines for yogurt; check expiration date on carton).

Makes about 1¼ cups

Calories per tablespoon: 7.4
Fat per tablespoon: 0
Cholesterol per tablespoon: 0.2 mg.

RED WINE VINEGAR DRESSING

1 tablespoon Dijon-style mustard
3 tablespoons water
½ cup red wine vinegar
1 large clove garlic
1½ tablespoons finely chopped
    white onion (less than ¼ small
    onion)
¼ teaspoon freshly ground black
    pepper
⅛ teaspoon dried oregano

Makes about ¾ cup

Calories per tablespoon: 3.9
Fat per tablespoon: 0.1 g.
Cholesterol per tablespoon: 0

Although created as a dressing, this tangy mixture imparts a wonderful flavor to red meat or game (apply before cooking and use to baste).

In a bowl, whisk together mustard and water. Whisk in vinegar. Using a garlic press, crush in garlic. Add remaining ingredients and mix thoroughly.

Suggested pairings: green salads, sliced chilled vegetables, sliced cold roast beef

This dressing may be stored in the refrigerator for up to three days.

MUSTARD VINAIGRETTE

4 tablespoons stone-ground
    mustard
1 teaspoon white wine vinegar
¼ teaspoon freshly ground black
    pepper
½ teaspoon Worcestershire sauce
1½ tablespoons water

Makes about ⅓ cup

Calories per tablespoon: 12.1
Fat per tablespoon: 0.7 g.
Cholesterol per tablespoon: 0

True to its name, this delicious dressing has mustard and vinegar—but none of the oil that puts many versions of the classic dressing out of bounds for the calorie conscious. This recipe can easily be cut in half or doubled.

Place mustard in a small bowl and whisk in vinegar. Whisk in pepper, then Worcestershire sauce, then water. Serve at room temperature or chilled (cover if chilling).

Suggested pairings: green salads, cold tuna or salmon

This dressing may be stored in the refrigerator for up to five days.

7
SALSAS, CHUTNEYS, AND STOCKS

BLACK BEAN SALSA
TOMATO SALSA
PEAR MANGO CHUTNEY
CRANBERRY MOCK CHUTNEY
PEACH CHUTNEY
BARBECUE MARINADE
HOMEMADE CHICKEN STOCK
HOMEMADE BEEF STOCK

BLACK BEAN SALSA

1 cup canned black beans, drained and rinsed under cold water
2 tablespoons coarsely chopped white onion (less than ¼ small onion)
1½ teaspoons minced garlic (about 2 cloves)
⅛ teaspoon dried oregano
¼ teaspoon ground cumin
2 teaspoons chopped fresh cilantro
¾ teaspoon freshly squeezed lime juice

Makes about 1¼ cups

Calories per tablespoon: 11.9
Fat per tablespoon: 0
Cholesterol per tablespoon: 0

This nutritious salsa can add a zesty southwestern flavor to almost any meat.

In a bowl, mix together black beans and onion. Add remaining ingredients and thoroughly mix together. Let stand at least 1 hour before serving to allow the flavors to blend together. Serve at room temperature or chilled (cover if chilling).

Suggested pairings: broiled fish, roast pork, cold poached chicken

This salsa may be stored in the refrigerator for up to three days.

TOMATO SALSA

1 tablespoon coarsely chopped
   fresh jalapeño pepper (see
   directions below) (about ⅓–½
   pepper)
1 cup diced fresh tomato (about 1
   tomato)
2 tablespoons coarsely chopped
   white onion (less than ¼ small
   onion)
1½ teaspoons minced garlic (about
   2 cloves)
⅛ teaspoon salt
¼ teaspoon dried oregano
1 tablespoon chopped fresh
   cilantro
¾ teaspoon freshly squeezed lime
   juice

Makes about 1¼ cups

Calories per tablespoon: 2.2
Fat per tablespoon: 0
Cholesterol per tablespoon: 0

This lively salsa can deliciously accompany both main courses and appetizers. It's particularly good with cold chicken cubes, baked taco chips, and toasted pita triangles. Carefully follow the instructions noted below for handling the jalapeño pepper.

Wearing rubber gloves, remove the stem from the pepper and cut the pod in half lengthwise. Remove all seeds and veins from inside. Hold pod under cold running water to be sure it is free of seeds. Coarsely chop pepper and set aside.
   Place tomato and onion into a bowl and mix well. Add pepper, garlic, salt, oregano, cilantro, and lime juice, thoroughly mixing all ingredients together. Let stand at least 1 hour before serving to allow the flavors to blend. Serve at room temperature or chilled (cover if chilling).

Suggested pairings: chicken, turkey, sole, whitefish

This salsa may be stored in the refrigerator for up to two days.

PEAR MANGO CHUTNEY

2 16-ounce cans pears packed in
    water, drained and chopped
    coarse
¼ cup seedless raisins (any variety)
1 cup chopped white onion (about
    1 medium onion)
2 dried pear halves, chopped
1½ tablespoons dark brown sugar
    (not packed)
½ cup mango nectar
¼ cup tarragon vinegar
¼ teaspoon ground ginger
¼ teaspoon curry powder
⅛ teaspoon cayenne pepper

Serve as a relish, as a side dish, or over cream cheese as an appetizer.

Place all ingredients in a large heavy-bottomed saucepan. Mix well, and bring to a boil over medium heat. Turn heat down to low and simmer uncovered about 1 hour, until mixture has thickened and almost all liquid has dissipated. Stir occasionally to prevent the mixture from sticking. Serve at room temperature or chilled (cover if chilling).

Suggested pairings: chicken, pork, lamb

This chutney may be stored in the refrigerator for up to one week.

Makes about 3 cups

Calories per tablespoon: 14.0
Fat per tablespoon: 0
Cholesterol per tablespoon: 0

CRANBERRY MOCK CHUTNEY

2 cups fresh cranberries (slightly less than 1 12-ounce bag)
1 large navel orange, peeled, cut into eighths, and seeded
1 large tart green apple, peeled, cut into eighths, and cored
2 tablespoons dark brown sugar (not packed)
1 tablespoon orange juice (fresh, if possible)
½ teaspoon ground ginger
1 tablespoon finely chopped candied ginger
1 tablespoon coarsely grated white onion
1 teaspoon grated lemon peel

Makes about 2¾ cups

Calories per tablespoon: 7.9
Fat per tablespoon: 0
Cholesterol per tablespoon: 0

This relish has the tartness and ginger undertaste of a chutney without requiring cooking. It makes for a savory condiment or side dish.

Place cranberries, orange, and apple in the bowl of a food processor or a blender. Pulse about 20 times, until coarsely chopped (or coarsely chop by hand). Transfer to a bowl, add remaining ingredients, and thoroughly mix all together. Let stand at least 1 hour before serving to allow the flavors to blend. Serve at room temperature.

Suggested pairings: sliced turkey or chicken, roast pork, ham, chilled smoked fish

This chutney may be stored in the refrigerator for up to five days.

PEACH CHUTNEY

1 16-ounce can peaches packed in
    water, drained and chopped
2½ dried peach halves, chopped
2½ extra large pitted prunes or 3–4
    small pitted prunes, chopped
    fine
½ tablespoon coarsely grated
    lemon peel
1 tablespoon freshly squeezed
    lemon juice
1 tablespoon finely chopped
    candied ginger
¼ teaspoon ground ginger
2 tablespoons tarragon vinegar
6 tablespoons white vinegar
1 tablespoon dark brown sugar
    (not packed)

Savory and slightly tart, this chutney works equally well us a relish for main courses or teamed up with appetizer-sized portions of food.

Combine all ingredients except brown sugar in a heavy-bottomed saucepan. Mix well, and bring to a boil over medium heat. Stir in brown sugar. Turn heat down to low and simmer uncovered for 30 to 40 minutes, stirring occasionally to prevent scorching, until chutney has thickened. Serve at room temperature or chilled (cover if chilling).

Suggested pairings: lamb, pork, chicken, shrimp

This chutney may be stored in the refrigerator for up to one week.

Makes about 2 cups

Calories per tablespoon: 10.3
Fat per tablespoon: 0
Cholesterol per tablespoon: 0

BARBECUE MARINADE

¼ cup chopped scallion (about 2–3 scallions, white and light green parts only)

3 tablespoons tomato paste

2 tablespoons red wine vinegar

2 teaspoons Worcestershire sauce

⅛ teaspoon hot sauce

¼ teaspoon chopped fresh jalapeño pepper

½ teaspoon ground coriander

3 cloves garlic

3½ tablespoons warm water

Makes about ⅔ cup

Calories per tablespoon: 5.7
Fat per tablespoon: 0
Cholesterol per tablespoon: 0

To marinate meats, place marinade and meat in a resealable plastic bag and refrigerate for at least 2 hours, turning once. When chopping the jalapeño pepper, be sure to wear rubber gloves, and remove and discard all seeds and veins from the pepper.

In a bowl, thoroughly mix together all ingredients except garlic and water. Using a garlic press, crush in garlic, and mix. Add water. Mix together all ingredients.

Suggested pairings: beef tenderloin, chicken

This marinade may be stored in the refrigerator for up to three days.

HOMEMADE CHICKEN STOCK

½ stewing chicken, cut in half or
   in pieces
5 carrots, trimmed and cut into
   chunks (unpeeled)
2 or 3 parsnips, trimmed and cut
   into chunks (unpeeled)
1 medium onion, peeled and cut
   into chunks
5 stalks celery, trimmed
¼ cup fresh parsley or 1
   tablespoon dried parsley
Water to cover 2 inches above
   ingredients (about 20 cups)
Salt to taste
Black pepper to taste

Makes about 1⅔ quarts

We recommend making large quantities of stock at a time and freezing ½ cup portions in reseulable plastic bags.

Place chicken, carrots, parsnips, onion, celery, and parsley in a large stockpot. Cover with water. Bring to a rapid boil over high heat. Skim foamy residue off the top. Turn heat down to low and simmer uncovered for 3 to 4 hours, periodically skimming the residue off the top, until chicken falls off bones when speared with a fork.

Take the pot off the hot burner. Remove and discard all solid ingredients from stock, and strain liquid into a large bowl. Add salt and pepper. Refrigerate uncovered for at least 2 to 3 hours. If refrigerating overnight, cover the bowl after 2 to 3 hours.

Using a large spoon, lift off as much of the layer of fat that has settled on top as possible. Using a dinner knife, scrape along the top of the stock to catch any additional small pieces of fat. Place the stock back into a large pot and cook over medium heat for 2 to 3 minutes, until it has turned from a gelatinous state back into liquid. Pour liquefied stock through a strainer lined with a double layer of cheesecloth (to strain sediment) into a clean bowl. The result is a flavorful, clear, fat-free broth.

This stock may be stored in the refrigerator for up to three days, or in the freezer for up to six months.

HOMEMADE BEEF STOCK

1 tablespoon canola oil
2-pound beef knuckle soup bone
    with meat (knuckle should be
    cracked open; if not
    prepackaged, make sure
    butcher has done so)
2 pounds beef marrow bones
2 stalks celery with leaves, broken
    in half
1 very large carrot, trimmed and
    broken in half (unpeeled)
1 large white onion, peeled
14 cups water
½ teaspoon salt
12 whole black peppercorns
1 large clove garlic, peeled

_____

Makes about 1 quart

The darker you brown the beef bones, the darker the color of this flavorful stock.

Pour oil into a large stockpot. Using a square of wax paper, coat the bottom and lower sides of the pot with the oil. Heat oil for 1 to 2 minutes over medium-high heat. Add bones and brown on all sides. Add celery, carrot, and onion. Pour in water, then add salt, peppercorns, and garlic. Bring to a boil over high heat. Turn heat down to low and simmer uncovered for 4 hours, periodically skimming the foamy residue off the top. Take the pot off the hot burner. Remove and discard all solid ingredients from stock, and strain liquid into a large bowl. Let cool. Refrigerate uncovered at least 2 to 3 hours. If refrigerating overnight, cover the bowl after 2 to 3 hours.

Using a large spoon, lift off as much of the layer of fat that has settled on top as possible. Using a dinner knife, scrape along the top of the stock to catch any additional small pieces of fat. Put the stock back into a large pot and cook over medium heat for 2 to 3 minutes, until it has turned from a gelatinous state back into liquid. Pour liquefied stock through a strainer lined with a double layer of cheesecloth (to strain sediment) into a clean bowl. The result is a delicious, clear, fat-free broth.

This stock may be stored in the refrigerator for up to three days, or in the freezer for up to six months.

8
DESSERT SAUCES

PASSION FRUIT MANGO SAUCE
PINEAPPLE APPLE COULIS
BLUEBERRY PEACH SAUCE
PAPAYA APRICOT SAUCE
LEMON DESSERT SAUCE
STRAWBERRY SAUCE
APRICOT SAUCE
TART CHERRY PEAR SAUCE
SWEET CHERRY SAUCE
RASPBERRY DESSERT SAUCE
COCOA RASPBERRY SAUCE

PASSION FRUIT MANGO SAUCE

½ cup passion fruit (pulpy insides, including seeds, of about 4 ripe passion fruits, shells discarded)
½ teaspoon powdered sugar
1 tablespoon mango nectar

Makes about ½ cup

Calories per tablespoon: 10.7
Fat per tablespoon: 0.1 g.
Cholesterol per tablespoon: 0

Be sure to use ripe passion fruit, which is somewhat puckered on the surface. If the passion fruit is smooth-skinned when purchased, allow it to ripen unrefrigerated for a few days.

Place passion fruit and powdered sugar in the bowl of a food processor or a blender. While pouring in nectar through the feed tube, puree to a smooth consistency. Cover and chill. Serve chilled.

Suggested pairings: pound cake, fresh berries, frozen yogurt

This sauce may be stored in the refrigerator for up to two days.

PINEAPPLE APPLE COULIS

1 8-ounce can crushed pineapple
    packed in natural juices
¼ cup water
¼ cup orange juice (fresh, if
    possible)
1 teaspoon grated orange peel
1 cup peeled, cored, and diced tart
    green apple (about 1 apple)

Makes about 1½ cups

Calories per tablespoon: 10.0
Fat per tablespoon: 0
Cholesterol per tablespoon: 0

A dessert sauce at heart, this thick, rich treat also goes nicely with roast pork or broiled fish.

Place all ingredients in a saucepan and mix together. Bring to a boil over medium heat. Turn heat down to low and simmer uncovered for about 20 minutes, stirring occasionally. Let cool. Serve at room temperature.

Suggested pairings: frozen yogurt, ice cream, pound cake

This sauce may be stored in the refrigerator for up to five days.

BLUEBERRY PEACH SAUCE

1 cup whole blueberries (fresh or
    unsweetened frozen)
1 tablespoon peach nectar
1 tablespoon freshly squeezed
    lemon juice
¼ teaspoon cinnamon
1 teaspoon powdered sugar

Makes about ¾ cup

Calories per tablespoon: 8.8
Fat per tablespoon: 0
Cholesterol per tablespoon: 0

This sauce holds up so well it can be made days in advance and refrigerated, with no decline in flavor or appearance. Garnish with whole blueberries or thinly sliced citrus rind.

Puree all ingredients to a smooth consistency in a food processor or blender. Cover and chill. Serve chilled.

Suggested pairings: frozen yogurt, sliced melon, yogurt cheesecake

This sauce may be stored in the refrigerator for up to five days.

PAPAYA APRICOT SAUCE

2 tablespoons papaya nectar
1 16-ounce can apricots packed in
    water, drained
½ teaspoon freshly squeezed lemon
    juice
½ tablespoon powdered sugar

Makes about 1¼ cups

Calories per tablespoon: 4.7
Fat per tablespoon: 0
Cholesterol per tablespoon: 0

This quick and easy sauce can be prepared just before dinner, chilled during dinner, and ready in time for dessert. Garnish with thinly sliced citrus rind, strawberry slices, or edible flowers.

Puree all ingredients to a smooth consistency in a food processor or blender. Cover and chill. Serve chilled.

Suggested pairings: frozen desserts, pound cake, melon

This sauce may be stored in the refrigerator for up to five days, or in the freezer for up to two weeks.

LEMON DESSERT SAUCE

½ tablespoon sugar
½ cup water
¼ cup freshly squeezed lemon juice
½ tablespoon chopped lemon peel
2 teaspoons cornstarch dissolved
   in 1 tablespoon water

Makes about ⅔ cup

Calories per tablespoon: 5.7
Fat per tablespoon: 0
Cholesterol per tablespoon: 0

Don't use a white pan when cooking this sauce, or it will be very difficult to tell when the sugar has dissolved. Garnish with sliced strawberry.

In a heavy-bottomed saucepan, heat sugar and water over medium heat, stirring constantly, until sugar is dissolved (1 to 2 minutes). Take care not to boil the mixture. Add lemon juice and peel, and stir. Continue to cook another 2 minutes. Whisk in cornstarch mixture. Cook an additional 2 minutes, whisking constantly. Let cool. Serve at room temperature.

Suggested pairings: melon, pound cake, chocolate angel food cake

This sauce may be stored in the refrigerator for up to two days.

STRAWBERRY SAUCE

1 cup whole strawberries (fresh or unsweetened frozen)
½ tablespoon powdered sugar
½ tablespoon freshly squeezed lemon juice

Makes about 1 cup

Calories per tablespoon: 3.8
Fat per tablespoon: 0
Cholesterol per tablespoon: 0

Straightforward and refreshing—a perennial favorite. Garnish with a twist of lemon rind or a sprig of fresh mint.

Puree all ingredients to a smooth consistency in a food processor or blender. Cover and chill. Serve chilled.

Suggested pairings: angel food cake, ice milk, sliced melon

This sauce may be stored in the refrigerator for up to two days.

APRICOT SAUCE

1 16-ounce can apricots packed in
    water, drained
½ cup apricot nectar
½ teaspoon freshly squeezed lemon
    juice

Makes about 1½ cups

Calories per tablespoon: 5.5
Fat per tablespoon: 0
Cholesterol per tablespoon: 0

This silky dessert sauce has an intense, robust flavor. It's good on roast veal as well as desserts.

Place apricots in the bowl of a food processor or blender. Add nectar and lemon juice. Puree to a smooth consistency. Serve at room temperature or chilled (cover if chilling).

Suggested pairings: vanilla yogurt, baked apple, pound cake

This sauce may be stored in the refrigerator for up to five days, or in the freezer for up to two weeks.

TART CHERRY PEAR SAUCE

1 cup whole pitted sour cherries
(fresh or canned packed in
water; if canned, slightly less
than 1 16-ounce can, drained)
1 teaspoon powdered sugar
2 tablespoons pear nectar

Makes about 1 cup

Calories per tablespoon: 7.1
Fat per tablespoon: 0
Cholesterol per tablespoon: 0

Despite its principal ingredient, this sauce is more sweet than tart, and can be deliciously paired with roast pork or game birds, as well as desserts.

Put cherries and sugar in the bowl of a food processor or a blender. While pouring in nectar through the feed tube, puree to a smooth consistency. Cover and chill to top desserts, or serve at room temperature with entrees.

Suggested pairings: baked apple, frozen yogurt

This sauce may be stored in the refrigerator for up to five days.

SWEET CHERRY SAUCE

¾ cup whole pitted dark sweet
   cherries (fresh or unsweetened
   frozen)
½ tablespoon powdered sugar
1 teaspoon freshly squeezed lemon
   juice
3 tablespoons water

Makes about ⅔ cup

Calories per tablespoon: 10.7
Fat per tablespoon: 0.1 g.
Cholesterol per tablespoon: 0

Garnish this flavorful sauce with whole sweet cherries and a slice of citrus peel, which stands out against the dark rich color.

Put cherries, sugar, and lemon juice in the bowl of a food processor or a blender. While adding water through the feed tube, puree to a smooth consistency. Cover and chill. Serve chilled.

Suggested pairings: frozen desserts, sliced fruit

This sauce may be stored in the refrigerator for up to five days.

RASPBERRY DESSERT SAUCE

1 cup whole raspberries (fresh or
  unsweetened frozen)
½ tablespoon powdered sugar
½ tablespoon freshly squeezed
  lemon juice

Makes about 1 cup

Calories per tablespoon: 4.8
Fat per tablespoon: 0
Cholesterol per tablespoon: 0

We like this refreshing sauce with its seeds intact, but you can strain it through a fine-mesh sieve if you prefer it seedless. For an elegant touch, garnish with fresh mint or a small amount of crumbled biscotti (an Italian cookie).

Puree all ingredients to a smooth consistency in a food processor or blender. Cover and chill. Serve chilled.

Suggested pairings: melon, sliced peaches, chocolate cake, custard

This sauce may be stored in the refrigerator for up to three days.

COCOA RASPBERRY SAUCE

½ cup whole raspberries (fresh or unsweetened frozen)
¾ teaspoon powdered sugar
¾ teaspoon freshly squeezed lemon juice
½ tablespoon cocoa powder

Makes about ½ cup

Calories per tablespoon: 5.7
Fat per tablespoon: 0.1 g.
Cholesterol per tablespoon: 0

A melding of two of America's favorite flavors. Try serving this sauce with cubes of frozen angel food cake or your favorite low-calorie cookie.

Puree all ingredients to a smooth consistency in a food processor or blender. Cover and chill. Serve chilled.

Suggested pairings: frozen yogurt, ice cream custard, lemon tart

This sauce may be stored in the refrigerator for up to two days.

INDEX